Successful Presenting

This book should be returned to any branch of the
Lancashire County Library on or before the date

Lancashire County Library
Bowran Street
Preston PR1 2UX

www.lancashire.gov.uk/libraries

further their careers. Lear
in a lifetime.

David Brown studied mechanical engineering at Loughborough University and secured a Diploma in Management Studies from the University of Aston.

David has over 30 years' experience of presenting as a manager and as a seller. For 15 years he worked as a senior manager for Alcan and Alumax, two multinational North American mining and metal businesses. For the past 22 years he has run his own business, acting as a consultant and coach specialising in improving business performance. More recently he has secured a diploma in neuro-linguistic programming (NLP), which has given him added insight into behaviours associated with effective communicating and presenting. In this book he shares with you the secrets of successful presenting in its many forms. For more information visit www.scott-brown.co.uk

Successful Presenting

David Brown

www.inaweek.co.uk

Teach Yourself®

IN A WEEK

Hodder Education

338 Euston Road, London NW1 3BH

Hodder Education is an Hachette UK company

First published in UK 2012 by Hodder Education

First published in US 2012 by The McGraw-Hill Companies, Inc.

British Library Cataloguing in Publication Data: a catalogue record for this title is available from the British Library.

Library of Congress Catalog Card Number: on file.

10 9 8 7 6 5 4 3 2 1

Hachette UK's policy is to use papers that are natural, renewable and recyclable products and made from wood grown in sustainable forests. The logging and manufacturing processes are expected to conform to the environmental regulations of the country of origin.

www.hoddereducation.co.uk

Typeset by Cenveo Publisher Services.

Printed in Great Britain by CPI Cox & Wyman, Reading.

Contents

Introduction

In an increasingly competitive world people are looking for something that makes a difference. This book is designed to help you to be perceived as making a difference – whether you operate within your own organization, or are generating business with a customer. When you pick up this book you might already consider yourself to be a success. You may be a competent presenter, but I hope you would accept that when it comes to communicating ideas to other people there is always room for improvement. Whether you are successful or competent, a beginner or an expert, there is something in this book that will help you achieve more in business through successfully communicating your messages. During the week I will offer you dozens of tips, some to do with strategy, some concerned with detail. All I promise you is that if you start with an attitude of mind that says, 'I can continuously improve my performance when presenting,' then at the end of the week you will feel it's been time well spent.

In the first two chapters we will look at two ideas that underpin successful business and successful presenting. Sunday looks at the concept of 'Start with the end goal in mind'; this is essential if you are to succeed as a businessperson and presenter. This approach is not easily switched on when you decide to present – it works best when all your business thinking is driven by what you want to finish up with. Monday, 'Recognize when you are presenting', is again a prerequisite to successful presenting; if you restrict your use of presentation skills to stand-up situations, you will be missing many other opportunities to use those skills to your advantage. Your skills should be second nature to you, and used in a wide variety of situations as you go about your daily business.

With your thinking underpinned by this solid foundation, during the rest of the week we will address the specific business of delivering effective presentations.

As a coach I am often approached to run workshops in 'advanced presenting'. I don't believe there is such a subject. Presenting is not that complicated – some presenters are simply better than others at using techniques that apply as much to the expert as to the novice. Many 'advanced presenters' that I coach already consider themselves to be expert. They might talk well; they might look flashy; but often they don't achieve their presentation objectives. However, if you are able to apply the tips in this book, you will present with confidence and be perceived as an effective and successful presenter.

SUNDAY

Start with the end goal in mind

You may have an unhelpful picture in your head of presenting being about someone standing in front of a group, supported by PowerPoint slides, sounding impressive and using big words.

I aim to show you that such an image could represent poor presenting, and many missed opportunities to use your presenting skills. I am going to show you that you present more often than you think you do. Most importantly, your success is governed by what you hope to achieve – the end that you have in mind. As a young manager, I thought that getting things done was important. It is, but it is not as important as doing the *right* things. In practice, this means *not* being driven by what is in your email inbox, but by remembering what you want to finish up with – your objective.

So, 'Start with the end goal in mind' is the most important concept in this book. It is infinitely more important than any tip or technique. That's why it's our first chapter.

What would prove that you are a good presenter? Surely, one of the most important criteria is that you should achieve your chosen goals, aims, objectives or outputs. (In the interests of variety we will use these terms as if they are freely interchangeable, much as the people you work with do.) So, let's have a look at one of the leading authorities on success, Stephen Covey, and the sorts of situations in which you need to present ideas in order to secure your goals.

Stephen Covey's book *The 7 Habits of Highly Effective People* is essential reading for anyone seeking to succeed more often. It's his habit no. 2 that I want to work with in this chapter – 'Begin with the end in mind'. When we present anything, if we focus on what we want to finish up with at the end, we are more likely to do appropriate things at the start! This is about putting less emphasis on what you do than on where you want to finish up. I have seen so many presenters obsessed with what they must do – use a slide, use PowerPoint, include a particular story, stand in a particular place, etc. However, the effective presenter constantly bears in mind the outputs required, and works flexibly with their audience to secure those outputs.

This is our first chapter because 'starting with the end in mind' should be your mentality in business whatever you are doing. Covey didn't just have presenting in mind when he came up with his seven habits. He feels (and I see this every day) that business success is much easier to achieve if the end goals are clear. Too often people become consumed by the task, and run around like headless chickens, especially in these pressurized, challenging times. Whatever activity you are engaged in, a regular reappraisal of what your ultimate goals are will make your priorities clearer, eliminate irrelevant activity and make success more likely.

Visualize success

If you start to question your ability to make a difference, think of positive things and remember the words of Mahatma Ghandi, 'If you think you are too small to make a difference, try spending the night with a mosquito.'

One of the best ways of managing your nerves and increasing your confidence is to visualize success. In a sense it's another way of starting with the end in mind. Top golfers don't just warm up on the range – they picture themselves hitting specific shots with specific clubs, and visualize a successful trajectory and a successful outcome. This is a key idea in neuro-linguistic programming (NLP) – we will return to this idea as part of your continuous improvement on Saturday.

If I said to you, 'Whatever you do, don't think of Mickey Mouse', what sort of image will you have in your mind? Correct. Mickey Mouse! If I say to you, 'Whatever you do when you present, don't get nervous,' then if you weren't nervous to start with, you will be now. The trick is to think positive things and picture positive images. So:

- Picture yourself standing tall in front of your audience.
- Imagine yourself handling questions with confidence.
- Picture your audience smiling at you and nodding in agreement.
- Picture everything that will contribute to you succeeding and you will be well on your way.

Where you might want to finish up

What sort of outcomes do you want from the various business situations in which you might find yourself presenting?

1 **In a meeting**, you might want to:
   - Enable others to understand your future plans.
   - Fully explain one of your decisions.
   - Gather opinions.
   - Change the way others feel about something; change them from state A to state B.
   - Agree action.
   - Sell products or services.
   - Seek to persuade others. (My favourite definition of selling is 'persuading a prospect to make a decision in your favour').
   - Sell an idea.

2 **When meeting with your boss**, you could surely seek to do all of the above. Read the list in number 1 again, and consider a few more things you may want to persuade your boss to do:
   - Give you a pay rise.
   - Release you to a new project.
   - Appraise your performance.
   - Support your personal development plans.

3 **In a one-on-one meeting with a fellow team member**, you may do the following instinctively, without even realizing that you are doing them:
   - Agree how to approach another department.
   - Overcome some differences between the two of you.
   - Decide how to present an idea to your boss.
   - Develop a mutual understanding.

4 **At a retirement presentation**, whether it is you or someone else doing the presenting, it is necessary to:
- Have everybody remember what a contribution the retiree has made.
- Help everyone visualize all the good things that you have done together.
- Generate a spirit that involves the whole gathering wishing the individual a healthy and happy retirement.

You are presenting more often than you realize

I have given you just four different scenarios. You are involved in dozens more as you go about your business. The common link in all these business situations is that you seek to achieve a specific output. You are presenting your ideas. People are presenting ideas back to you. You might not always use PowerPoint – sometimes you might show someone an article in a journal to support your point. You might not be standing; you might be sitting down You might have two hours, or you might have 30 seconds. One thing is sure: as you go about your everyday business you are using presentational skills in myriad different ways to ensure that you succeed in business. You are 'presenting' more often than you realize.

This book is crammed with tips on how to present successfully. Your job is to become comfortable with all these possibilities, but first to *realize when you are presenting*. Only then will you be able to pick and choose the right options and the right style to suit each situation in which you find yourself presenting.

Summary

Far too many people are preoccupied with action – what they have to do. This is true of making effective presentations, but is also an important idea for all aspects of business life. We will regularly return to the question of how important your audience is, but you will only succeed with them if you follow the advice of Stephen Covey: always 'start with the end in mind'. *Think outputs!* This will help you understand the big picture, help you avoid being preoccupied with the subject, and help you think strategically. This in turn will increase your chances of being successful with each presentation and each business initiative.

Now try some multiple-choice questions. For some of these questions, there is more than one correct answer, but the most powerful response, the one that will help you succeed, is given in the answers at the end of the book.

MONDAY

TUESDAY

WEDNESDAY

THURSDAY

FRIDAY

SATURDAY

Questions

1. If your presentation is to succeed, you should be driven by:
   a) eye-catching visuals ☐
   b) a sophisticated projection system ☐
   c) the audience being impressed by you ☐
   d) what you want to achieve – the end you have in mind. ☐

2. The most important element of your presentation is:
   a) clarity about the outputs you seek ☐
   b) the beginning ☐
   c) the middle ☐
   d) the end. ☐

3. At the end of your presentation, you want your audience to be impressed by:
   a) you ☐
   b) your language ☐
   c) your material ☐
   d) what you want them to do, feel or know. ☐

4. What style should you adopt?
   a) One that suits you personally, whether that is formal or informal. ☐
   b) One that suits your final goal. ☐
   c) One that suits your audience. ☐
   d) One that is most used by presenters within the organization that you are presenting to. ☐

5. You will be perceived as a good presenter if you:
   a) achieve your chosen goals ☐
   b) look good ☐
   c) talk well ☐
   d) use fancy kit. ☐

6. What should all your presentations have in common?
   a) A clear purpose which you never lose sight of. ☐
   b) They should be short. ☐
   c) They should be lengthy. ☐
   d) They should be of a flexible duration. ☐

7. How often do you present?
   a) Only when you are asked to. ☐
   b) Only when you stand up. ☐
   c) Only when you are in front of two or more people. ☐
   d) More often than you realize! ☐

8. How long do you have to 'present'?
   a) 60 seconds ☐
   b) one hour ☐
   c) ten minutes ☐
   d) Any of the above – you must be prepared to be flexible. ☐

9. The best way to achieve your objectives is to:
a) be super energetic ☐
b) flatter your audience ☐
c) tell them what they want to hear ☐
d) make sure they understand where you are heading – the end goal. ☐

10. How will you realize when you need to use your presentation skills?
a) Your boss will tell you to make a presentation. ☐
b) Someone will invite you to make a presentation. ☐
c) You are asked to use PowerPoint. ☐
d) By spotting that you are with a particular person, or people, that allow you to achieve clearly defined business objectives. ☐

SUNDAY

MONDAY

TUESDAY

WEDNESDAY

THURSDAY

FRIDAY

SATURDAY

MONDAY

Recognize when you are presenting

In this chapter I will define presenting, and continue with the theme that you are presenting more often than you realize, and sometimes presenting when you are not conscious of it. Armed with a definition you will move on to become even more aware of the many different situations in which you present, plus a few where you are being presented to.

After today, the rest of the week is about the attitude, skills and knowledge you need to present effectively, but before diving into such tips I want you to study the table of practical examples that follows. These, and dozens more situations like them, could apply to you as you go about your business and your personal life. As a result of appreciating the sort of communications you are involved in, you will be better able to realize when you are presenting. Then you will see how you can put to good use the tips in the rest of the book as you communicate on a one-to-one basis or with large groups, and how skilled presenting can become second nature to you.

There are as many definitions of presenting as there are people offering opinions on the subject. The definition that I offer is quite simple:

Successful presenting is communicating effectively with people in order to realize your objectives.

This is a very broad definition, but I put it to you because a narrow definition of presenting is likely to result in a bored audience and in you failing to communicate effectively. It is positively unhelpful for you to have an image of presenting as standing up, having 'the gift of the gab' and hiding behind (or standing in front of!) a PowerPoint presentation. If you recognize that the essence of succeeding in business is communicating successfully, with different techniques for different people, then you will present successfully to a wide range of audiences, you will enjoy it and you will succeed at it. The rest of this book tells you how to do it!

You present every day

So, let's look at the sort of objectives you might have, and how they might be relevant to you as you present. The list in the table below is by no means comprehensive, so I want you to keep asking yourself, 'Is there an element of presenting in what I am about to do? If so, how can I best use the tips in this book in this particular situation?' To help you in this process, I have also included a handful of situations in which others present to you.

When you are presenting	Outputs that are sought
At a team meeting	Team members are provided with information they clearly understand.
When liaising with another department	The other department's mind is changed on a procedure – change how they feel about it.
When you, the expert, are coaching one-on-one	The other person understands new technology, develops new skills/attitudes.
When selling a product or service	The other party buys what you had in mind.
When negotiating a contract	You reach agreement.
During a consultative process	You get ideas from others involved.

During a brainstorming session	You get ideas, or stimulate a reaction.
When you are asking for help; could be with anyone	The other person or people are motivated to help you.
When you are developing a better relationship with someone	They understand you or one of your interests. You understand them.
When you are presenting a budget for approval	The package is agreed.
In discussion with your manager	A decision is made.
In discussion with any group or individual	They move from feeling negative to positive about something you care about.
When someone is not co-operating with you	They are motivated to embrace a change. You develop a mutual understanding.
During a quick encounter in the corridor	The other party agrees to act in a particular way.
When offering a written report	Your findings are accepted.
When submitting your CV (another example of a written presentation)	You are offered an interview.
When attending a job interview	You are offered the job.
When giving a wedding speech	Your audience is entertained

When you are being presented to	Outputs that are sought
When you listen to the news on the radio	You know what's going on in the world.
When you watch a TV documentary	You acquire fresh knowledge.
When you attend a lecture	You are given knowledge.
When you are being trained	Your knowledge or skills are improved.
When you are being coached	Your skills or attitude are improved.
When you read this book	You succeed with presentations.

Not every situation requires presentation

Although I seek to show you that you present more often than you realize, there are some situations where it is not wise to present – if you feel ill equipped; if you have insufficient time to prepare; if your audience will not be receptive, or if a key authority cannot be present in the room. This latter case is particularly important, because if you are to succeed you need an audience with an appropriate mix of power and influence. Be aware that it's power that allows influence!

Whether in a formal or informal situation, you are 'presenting', and being presented to, for much of your business life – so realizing what is going on will help you manage each situation better, and help you secure maximum benefit from the rest of your week's study. One of the implications of understanding more about presenting is that you will also know when not to make too big an issue of something by elevating it to 'presentation' status – just sort it out by having a simple conversation, or dropping someone a line.

Having said this, the most serious problem that I see is not that people present when they shouldn't – it is that they fail to recognize when they should make use of their presentation skills.

I presented (not face to face, but over the telephone) to Hodder, the publishers of this book, a view as to how I would go about writing the book and why I should be commissioned to do it. As a reader of this book, aren't you lucky I realized my objective and they said 'Okay'?

Techniques and technology

We are going to move on to techniques for using your voice, body language, a raft of props such as visual aids (clips from YouTube, samples, models, photos) as well as projectors, laptops, touch-screen computers, TVs, flip charts, Kindles, iPods, and BlackBerrys to mention but a few. The point is that we can use these devices in all of the examples given in the table above, and in a whole lot more situations as well. The trick is to use the right thing at the right time. We will return to this regularly, but for today the message is that, to make best use of these communication aids, you first need to realize that you are presenting!

Realize when you are presenting and you will be well placed to decide which of the tips in this book to use. I am not suggesting that you should use all of the tips all of the time – only that an awareness of when you are presenting, and when you are being presented to, will help you to successfully manage each business situation. You will recognize the many different situations in which you are presenting, and appreciate how the communication techniques looked at in this book can be an important part of your everyday skill set.

I cannot stress too strongly how most of the tips in this book can help your communication with individuals on a one-to-one basis as much as your work with large groups. Of course, the idea that you should scan an entire room does not apply to your one-to-one communication – but the vast majority of the tips will be useful to you if you adapt them to suit the situation. Here's a tip that links large groups, small groups, and one-to-ones: 'Condense your objectives, or outputs (such as those in the table above), into a single sentence which will focus you on the task, for example: I want to stimulate the other party so that when we have finished they want to sit down with me one-on-one to discuss how this helps them.' The added focus will help you prepare effectively (we will look at this tomorrow); it's also another example of how starting with the end in mind will work for you!

Summary

It's very easy to be obsessed with your message, the visual aids you use, delivery techniques and the mechanics of presenting. Most people fall into this trap; they think these things are all-important when they are not, and this notion puts them under pressure. They ask themselves, 'Have I got this right?', 'Should I stand up or sit down?' If they only 'started with the end in mind' and linked this with realizing when they are presenting, the pressure would be lifted and they would present quite naturally.

We will consider the importance of your audience on **Tuesday** and **Thursday**. Even at this stage, it is worth linking these ideas to future chapters, because understanding your audience is another priority if your presentations are to be well received. We will see that considering your audience is an essential part of taking the pressure off yourself, which makes it more important than which prop to use, or what presenting technique to employ.

SUNDAY

MONDAY

TUESDAY

WEDNESDAY

THURSDAY

FRIDAY

SATURDAY

The point of this chapter, however, is that for you to make appropriate decisions about anything on this subject, you first need to realize when you are presenting. Then, as you go about your daily business, you can develop a wide range of presentation skills to communicate effectively and achieve your goals more often.

Questions

1. 'Presenting' is:
   a) talking in front of a group of people ❏
   b) putting on a show ❏
   c) impressing one or more people ❏
   d) communicating effectively with people in order to achieve your objectives. ❏

2. What is the most important skill you need in order to present effectively?
   a) talking ❏
   b) communicating in a variety of different ways ❏
   c) looking smart ❏
   d) being organized ❏

3. To be a success in business you need to:
   a) realize when you are working with other people to achieve your chosen objectives, and draw on whatever presentation skills are needed for you to succeed ❏
   b) agree with everybody ❏
   c) challenge everybody ❏
   d) agree with your boss. ❏

4. What props might you need when you present?
   a) a flip chart ❏
   b) PowerPoint ❏
   c) handouts ❏
   d) all of these, and anything else that ensures you achieve your goals ❏

5. How will people know that you are presenting?
   a) You will be standing in front of them. ❏
   b) You will have set a formal time to start. ❏
   c) There is a formal seating arrangement. ❏
   d) They may not realize that you are presenting to them. (You may be the only one who realizes, yet you will achieve what you want.) ❏

6. What size of audience are you likely to present to?
   a) one person ❏
   b) six people ❏
   c) however many people you happen to be with when you realize that one of your business objectives is within your grasp ❏
   d) 56 people ❏

7. You should seek to present:
   a) at a set time ❏
   b) in a set place, such as a monthly team meeting ❏
   c) on any occasion, in a flexible way that is acceptable to those with whom you work, once you realize the opportunity to influence them is there ❏
   d) at any time, whether the other parties want to listen to you or not. ❏

8. When might you seize the opportunity to use your presentation skills?
a) in a team meeting ☐
b) in a discussion with your manager ☐
c) when resolving conflict ☐
d) in all these situations, and a lot more besides ☐

9. When might you miss an opportunity to present, without realizing it?
a) when you're asked to ☐
b) when you bump into someone in the corridor, because this is when you may well be able to use one or two of the tips in this book to achieve one of your aims ☐
c) when you lack confidence ☐
d) when it is made quite clear to all concerned that it's down to you ☐

10. You should not present, even though you might have an opportunity to do so, when:
a) you can't be bothered ☐
b) you have had a difficult situation with a member of the audience ☐
c) there has been conflict over the subject, and you feel uncomfortable ☐
d) key people are missing from your audience. ☐

TUESDAY

Prepare!

I make no apologies for repeating my earlier messages. It is easy to skimp on preparation and charge straight into presenting. It's easy to rush into action and 'do'. It's so much more important to take time to be quite sure what your ultimate goal is – this drives your whole preparation.

Once you've understood this (see **Sunday**), and realized that you have an opportunity to present (see **Monday**), you need to prepare in three major areas: your audience, yourself and your material. We will consider other aspects of preparation, but these are the key areas. I've deliberately put them in that order, because in my experience people come unstuck by putting them in the reverse order. They start with what words to use, what visuals, which projector to use, and then they give some thought to their audience. I will show you why you should start your preparation by considering your audience. This will help you relate to them and engage with them, which is crucial if you are to achieve the results you want. Starting with the audience takes the pressure off you, and shows you why you and your material are not as important as you think.

It's your audience that has to be satisfied if you are to be successful, so that's why they come first!

Getting in the right frame of mind

Before we look at your audience, I just want to reinforce the idea of doing justice to preparation by sharing these quotes with you:

Proper preparation prevents poor performance.

This quote is attributed to almost as many people as there are experts on presentations. It's known as the five Ps.

Time spent on reconnaissance is rarely wasted.

This is attributed to a host of famous generals, including Napoleon, Wellington, Custer and Montgomery. The point I would make is that you are going into a sort of battle – and you want to do as much as possible to make sure that you win.

It takes one hour of preparation for each minute of presentation time.

Wayne Burgraff, 18th-century philosopher

I wouldn't offer this last quote to you as a fixed rule in the 21st century (because sometimes you will be able to prepare quickly), but would ask you to realize that an effective presentation is founded on more preparation time than delivery time.

You might think of your presentation as the tip of an iceberg. You only see it because of the nine tenths that is under the water. Your presentation will only stay afloat if there is solid preparation beneath it.

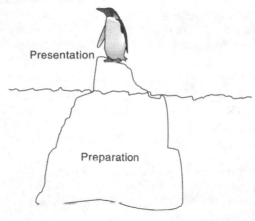

How to succeed with your presentation

Now you're sold on that, let's start with the audience.

Prepare for your specific audience

If you are to succeed, you need to enter the world of your audience. How many times has a specialist (such as an IT person) completely lost you? Mark Twain said, 'If you are to enter another person's shoes you must first take off your own.' So take off your shoes and enter the world of your audience! Then you will be well placed to meet their expectations of you, and succeed.

A great way to enter the world of your audience is to ask yourself lots of questions about them. If you don't know the answer, go and find it – then you will be much better equipped to work with them.

- How many people will there be?
- Where are they normally located?
- What are their priorities?
- How are they split? Are they young or old, managers or managed, receptive or hostile, experts on the subject or not?
- What will these different sections of your audience do with your ideas?

The above are fairly obvious. So too is the fact that you can't get to know everything about your audience. But you have to invest time in this if you are to avoid what I witnessed at a national conference of academics. The usually confident presenter was floored by some unexpected delegates turning up. Her conclusion was that she should have done a late check of who was going to be in the room, because that would have flagged up the awkward questions that were bound to be asked by certain people. Here are some more questions you might like to ask your audience:

- How would you sum them up in two or three words?
- How will they prefer to receive messages – verbally, visually, through activities, or through sharing emotions?
- Do they prefer theoretical or practical things, facts and figures or concepts?
- How much do they want to be there? Are they eager to attend, under duress, nervous or relaxed?
- How much time do they have?
- What language or jargon will they respond to best? Your favourite idea might be clear to you, but how will you make it as clear to your audience? A Treasury borrowing requirement of £50 billion probably means very little to you; increasing the standard rate of tax from 20p to 50p probably means more. So too would an explanation that the Treasury's woes are equivalent to a £1000 debt for every one of us. These all amount to the same thing! Express your idea in the terms that your audience will appreciate.
- What might they be biased towards or against?
- Are they united or divided?
- What is their culture? Different companies have different cultures. So too do different ethnic groups. Every group has its own culture, and you need to understand it – then respond to it.
- Will they respond favourably to you using their first names?
- What do they know now? What do they need to know?
- How will they dress?
- What examples and stories could you use to show them you are on the same wavelength as them?
- What obstacles do you have to overcome? Recognizing the obstacles allows you to put a plan in place to knock them down one by one.

Now you probably know more about your audience than you thought you did! Every one of your answers gives you a clue as to how you need to respond as you prepare yourself and assemble your material.

Prepare yourself

You don't drown by falling in the water.
You drown by staying there.

Anonymous

Whoever said this touched on a crucial aspect of presenting. Presenting formally is not a natural thing to do, so it is perfectly natural, even desirable, to start your presentation feeling nervous. So, don't expect to banish fear or nerves – what you have to do is manage them to stop yourself drowning. I prefer to call this 'controlling apprehension'. It's a very important part of managing nerves, so let's give it prominence.

Controlling apprehension

The best way to manage nerves is to prepare properly. Do this, and when you come to present, your nerves will be manageable.

● Prepare sufficiently so that you feel able to control the session.
● Accept that there is no simple remedy, and that some apprehension is natural and positive. It's only to do with adrenaline, which gives you energy. Avoid the temptation

to be comfortable; there does need to be a little edge. Ask yourself whether you need to calm down or fire yourself up.

- Plan to display courtesy and modesty rather than arrogance. Then you will be better able cope with the odd forgotten word with a shrug of the shoulders and 'excuse me'.
- Relate to the audience before and during your presentation. Take the pressure off yourself by thinking of them, and not you.
- Remember that your audience is not 'out to get you' unless you antagonize them.
- Be sure when you are offering *facts* and when you are offering *an idea* that might be debated. Decide how long you are prepared to debate an issue, and how you will move on after any questions or short discussion.
- See yourself as an authority, but not someone who knows all the answers.

- Learn to live with some ambiguity. Let things develop rather than insist they are rigid.
- Don't 'awfulize' things. Ask yourself what happens if something goes wrong, and you will realize that usually it is not that awful. Your audience will not be bothered if you are momentarily stuck for a word. They came for your bigger ideas, and they will not mind a pause.
- Make rehearsal count – if you can, gain prior access to the room. Move about the room (just as you will on the day); use all your kit; use all your material; stand up, sit down. Variety is best built in at the rehearsal stage. Rehearse out loud, because

you can get no sense of timing if you rehearse in your head. Then you will get a sense of whether you are varying your voice sufficiently. Variations in pitch, tone, volume and emphasis are a crucial part of keeping the attention of your audience. Experiment with changes of pace, which will retain attention.

- Don't over-rehearse or your boredom will show. Trust yourself!
- Don't take big risks with things you are unlikely to be comfortable with. Autocue, for instance, is something for which most people need considerable practice.

Rehearsal tip

To got the best out of your rehearsal, consider videoing yourself. Also, consider asking colleagues for feedback using the competent presenter checklist in **Saturday**. One item in this list is a check on your favourite words and mannerisms, things like 'uhm', 'er', 'actually', and involuntary twitches. As a ten-year-old, my daughter came home from school one day with an observation about how many times the headmaster had said 'very' during morning assembly 'Twenty-four today, Dad.' Unfortunately she couldn't tell me what else he'd said! No amount of words can reveal what you are doing as effectively as a video recorder; so video yourself. Then you can set about making sure that your mannerisms are within acceptable limits for your audience and allow your message to take centre stage.

- Find triggers that help you cope with pressure.
- Use memory aids rather than your memory (see **Friday**). Memorization is pressure! Forgetting where you are is also a pressure, but in my experience the greater pressure comes from thinking that you must remember. Your audience will be oblivious to much of what you think you must remember!
- Have strategies for dealing with the unexpected, such as interruptions (see **Friday**) or tricky questions (see **Thursday**).
- Be yourself. Don't expect to be perfect. You are okay!
- Choose clothes that you and your audience will be comfortable with.

- Use your own words, unless you choose to read a quote (don't try to remember a quote – there's no need).
- Aim to be conversational rather than clever with words. KISS (keep it simple, stupid) is what works best because simple language can convey complicated ideas in such a way that they are understood by all.

Coping with pressure

The New Zealand rugby team developed a reputation for failing under pressure, even though for many years they were considered the best team in the world. They put that right in the 2011 World Cup and, according to their coach Graham Henry, they were greatly helped by positive triggers. One player chose to tap his knee; another splashed his face with water; another stamped on the ground. They were all managing stress in their own way. (You could do a search on 'NLP anchors' for in-depth ideas on how to manage stressful situations.)

- Choose a comfortable stance, but vary it by moving around to help you relax.
- Decide whether you need to occupy your hands – with cue cards, a pointer, notes, a mouse. Variety is useful here, so that your audience is not aware of any one particular habit. Manage your nerves and this will not be an issue!
- Start with something that you are confident about. (See 'Purpose', 'Benefit' and 'Structure' on **Wednesday**.)
- Build in breaks and pauses to suit you. Pauses for a drink are okay. Pauses to allow reflection are also fine.
- Pick a time slot to suit you. Avoid the graveyard slot after lunch, when no one will be paying attention.
- Consider asking the audience to do something before you meet up: read an article; view a website; answer a question.
- Remember one of your good performances.
- Don't plan to impress – plan to succeed. Don't plan for them to remember you – plan for them to do what you want them to do, feel what you want them to feel.
- Above all, to manage nerves concentrate more on outcomes than on what you will do.

Ensure that the environment is right

You will become very nervous if you sense something is going wrong during your presentation, so you need to ensure that the environment is conducive to you getting your message across. Here are some of the things that you should consider before your presentation:

- Room size – it should not be too big or too cramped.
- Comfortable (friendly, if possible) seating. Try to avoid lecture style. A U style allows more interaction. We'll look at this on **Thursday** under 'Body language'.
- Temperature control – you don't want them to fall asleep in the warmth, or to freeze.
- The sun shining in – this can cause an uncomfortable glare and can warm up the room.
- Noise control – from movements of people, external traffic or air conditioning.
- Lighting – not too bright for your visuals, but bright enough to keep the audience awake.
- Tables for your equipment and props – make sure they are not positioned as a barrier between you and your audience.
- Distractions around the room – look out for and avoid things like pictures where you will be positioning flip charts that you will leave displayed.
- Anything that you need to suit you and the situation!

You should consider all these things beforehand, but come the day you need to monitor them and respond to any changes in a flexible way.

Some tips to help you immediately prior to delivery:

- Before you start, try tensing and relaxing any part of your body six times – your hands, thighs, face or neck. This can be done without anyone being aware of it, and helps to relieve tension.
- Before you start, warm up your voice. One tip is to sing – out of earshot of your audience!
- Before and during your presentation, breathe slowly and deeply from your abdomen, not from your lungs. If you slow down your breathing you will be in touch with your feelings and able to control them.
- Avoid caffeine, as it tenses your vocal chords. Water is the best lubricant.

Prepare your material

The audience only pays attention as long as you know where you are going.

Philip Crosby, Total Quality pioneer

Some people like to prepare using lists. My daughter always prepares using a Mind Map, which is a diagrammatic brainstorm. The longer I am in this business the more helpful I find Mind Maps as I try to organize my thoughts and my materials. Mind Maps will help you make sense of a complicated subject. They can be handwritten. The example that follows shows the factors involved in making a successful presentation. I often spread small sticky notes, with headings on them, over a large table, then shuffle them around until I feel comfortable with the whole picture. (That's how I planned this book.)

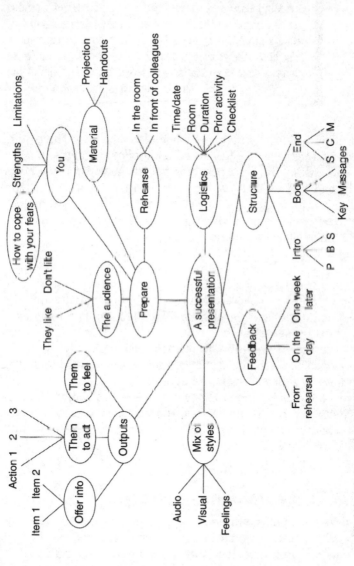

Mind Map: A successful presentation

You might like to consider your Mind Map as a tree. The core theme is the trunk; the key areas are the main boughs; the subsections are the branches. Whether you go as far as the twigs at the end is up to you and your assessment of the detail required.

You may prefer to think of your preparation as a road map that leads you to a particular destination. However you use this idea, make sure that the final destination is clear!

Mind Maps help me see the links between different parts of the big subject and help me decide what might be useful for my audience, and what I might discard. (Always start with too much material then ruthlessly thin it out to suit your purpose.) If you've never used a Mind Map, try using one on your next presentation.

You can access material from many sources today – your experience, the web, books, newspapers and journals to mention just a few. When you decide what to use and what to discard, do resist the temptation to copy large chunks straight into your presentation. This is plagiarism, and in any case your audience will expect to see ideas with your personal stamp on them. And they don't just want ideas, they want your interpretation of the ideas and, more importantly, how the ideas will affect them.

Vary your communication style

Now we'll look at the three communication styles that are defined in neuro-linguistic programming (NLP). NLP shows us that we communicate in three fundamental ways. Each of us has different preferences for these different forms of communication and, when you present, you need to appeal to an audience that will have a mix of preferences. The three communication styles are:

- **audio** – to do with *sound*, and what you say
- **visual** – what you *show* your audience
- **kinaesthetic** – a fancy word for *feelings* and emotions.

Remember that your audience will all be capable of receiving your messages in these three ways, but some will prefer to absorb the audio, some the visual and some the feelings. The key to successful presenting is to mix your material and your approach so that everybody stays tuned in.

Take an example of a safety officer making a presentation about the importance of abiding by the company's policy with regard to wearing safety shoes on the factory floor. Here is an example of what might appeal to the various people in the room.

Communication style	What you say or what you do
Audio	'If you don't wear safety shoes in this area you are likely to have a serious foot injury.'
Visual	Show a picture of a crushed safety shoe where the foot has escaped serious injury.
Feeling	Show a picture of a crushed, unprotected foot and ask the question, 'How would you like to go home to your family with this injury?'

I am not suggesting that you need to cover every point with all three styles of communication. There is no need to get technical about this – just ensure that your presentation has a mix that will strike a chord with everyone in your audience.

Finally, going back to these three styles, when you rehearse, imagine the scene:

- See what your audience will see. (You can video yourself.)
- Hear what your audience is likely to hear.
- Feel what your audience is likely to feel.

Then be flexible enough on the day to cope with the fact that reality is different from rehearsal. The function of rehearsal is not to predict everything, but to make sure you succeed come the day.

Choose your visual aids

During our week we will often look at visual aids and how to use them effectively. During your preparation you should consider how to use visual aids in your presentation, but keep an open mind about whether you will use a laptop, flip charts, projectors, videos, PowerPoint, models, brochures and so on. These are only a means to an end – they are not the essence of good presenting. They are only a part of you communicating in the three different styles mentioned above.

The best way to decide what support materials you need is to consider everything we have covered so far this week, then rehearse, then take stock of your approach before deciding what material you will use – and how.

If you always find yourself opting for the same approach with the same kit, you will get it wrong – because successful presenting comes from you having a special approach to a specific audience in a one-off situation. Another reason for challenging yourself if you find yourself opting for the same medium is that technology is moving all the time, and you need to move with it. It won't be long before your phone (or some other device) will allow you to control an image on the wall, have a laser-pointing device built in, have apps for different visual aids and apps for a host of memory aids to support you. The second you rely on one such device, you have lost it – because variety is essential if you are to keep your audience's attention.

Summary

You don't have to be flashy to be a good presenter. Thorough preparation is much more important than you being impressive. If you take on board the messages in this chapter, you will appeal to a business audience because you will help them towards their goals. Start with your audience, think about yourself, and only then move on to the material you will use and what you will use to get your messages across. If you prepare along the suggested lines you will take a great deal of pressure off yourself, because it will be clear to you and your audience that you are not the primary consideration – they are!

SUNDAY

MONDAY

TUESDAY

WEDNESDAY

THURSDAY

FRIDAY

SATURDAY

Questions

1. The most important aspect of preparation is:
a) you feeling comfortable ☐
b) not taking too long ☐
c) how to project your images ☐
d) understanding your objectives and your audience. ☐

2. Which of these are you most likely to skimp on in your preparation (if you are like most people that I've coached)?
a) your objectives ☐
b) your audience ☐
c) yourself ☐
d) your material ☐

3. What is the best language to use?
a) simple language ☐
b) the language of your audience ☐
c) whatever you are most comfortable with ☐
d) anything, so long as it makes you seem clever ☐

4. What should you do about nerves?
a) Pretend they are not there. ☐
b) Presume that they will go away. ☐
c) Carry a pack of cue cards to occupy your hands. ☐
d) Re-read today's notes on controlling apprehension. ☐

5. What does adequate rehearsal do for you?
a) It gives you a clear conscience. ☐
b) It allows you to get it word perfect. ☐
c) It equips you to be flexible enough to allow you to cope with anything that is thrown at you. ☐
d) It proves how clever you are. ☐

6. The most damaging thing that could happen to you is that you:
a) dry up ☐
b) forget a point you'd planned to make ☐
c) make a mistake over some statistic ☐
d) set off thinking how awful any of these things would be. ☐

7. The best way to rehearse is:
a) in the room with all the props you will use on the day ☐
b) on your own, to take the pressure off ☐
c) with your best friend boosting your confidence ☐
d) out of sight, in case anyone should realize that you need practice. ☐

8. Audience engagement starts when you:
a) arrange the session and send out your joining instructions ☐
b) stand up to begin your introduction ☐
c) use the first example that relates to them ☐
d) walk into the room. ☐

9. The best communication style to use is:
a) audio (verbal) ☐
b) visual (seen) ☐
c) kinaesthetic (feelings) ☐
d) an appropriate blend of all three. ☐

10. What is the best approach to visual aids?
a) Use the most recent technology. ☐
b) Rely on the spoken word. ☐
c) Use the most impressive display you can get hold of. ☐
d) Use a variety, a blend that will keep the attention of your audience. ☐

SUNDAY MONDAY TUESDAY WEDNESDAY THURSDAY FRIDAY SATURDAY

WEDNESDAY

Have a sound structure

Whether you are presenting within your organization or working with external customers, adopting these ideas on structure will allow you to stand out – mainly because so few people get this right. There is another reason why I know this will give you an edge; this framework has been the biggest single factor in improving the performance of the hundreds of people I have helped over the past 20 years. Why? It's simple: because a good structure retains attention and promotes understanding.

Most presenters are mistakenly obsessed with the material, and how they will deliver it. They are stuck on PowerPoint slides, impressive words, the body of their material being all-important, and too much focus on themselves. The structure that we will look at revolves around your objectives and how your audience will be persuaded by your case. An effective structure has an introduction, a main body and a clear end.

- The introduction engages the audience, shows them what's going to happen in the session, and allows the presenter to kick off with confidence.
- The body is something that most people have no trouble with, except they put too much in it.
- The end secures your objectives and leaves your audience in no doubt about why they came.

An easily understood structure is based on the old presentation motto of, 'Tell 'em, tell 'em, and tell 'em.' That is, tell them what you are going to tell them about; tell them about it; then tell them what you have told them. You might shudder and think this is repetition, but it is necessary when you consider that no one will listen to your every word, so you have to touch on the big issues more then once. When you next watch the TV news, notice how they use this principle. They tell you what the story is about, then tell you the story and finish with summary, conclusion or next steps – or maybe all three. They will keep your interest by varying the words and language in the introduction, the body and the end. Here's an example of how a ten-minute presentation could be structured.

A sound structure

Part	Approximate time
Introduction ● *Purpose* – explain why we are here. ● *Benefit* – tell the audience what's in it for them; why they should listen/get engaged. ● *Structure* – list the areas that you intend to cover – your agenda.Purpose, benefit and structure can be in any order. Choose the order that will have maximum impact on your audience.	Tell 'em 1 minute

Body
● This should be driven by your objectives/desired outcomes:
  – What do you want the audience to do?
  – What do you want the audience to feel?
● Have clear headings and signposts, aimed at your objectives.
● Stick to simple messages.
● Don't focus on your delivery! Focus on what is needed. Only use the material that you need to make your case.
	Tell 'em
	
	8 minutes

End ● *Summary* – extract the main points from each section. ● *Conclusion* – offer your *very personal* conclusion. ● *More* – explain what you want your audience to do next. Options may be a good idea here.	Tell 'em 1 minute

You can use your good sense to vary the times involved, but you need a three-part introduction before getting involved in any detail; then you need the body; then you need all three parts of the end to complete your case. No presentation is complete without all these elements.

Now let's have a look at each section in detail.

The introduction

Any introduction should have three parts, and below I offer you an example that relates to developing a business plan. (Say these three parts out loud It will take you less than a minute.)

1 **Purpose** – this is where you explain why you are together today. 'We're going to look at where we've got to with our business plan, and how we will finalize it.' (less than 10 seconds)

2 **Benefit** – your audience needs to know why they should bother to listen. So you need to tell them what's in it for them, and why they should get engaged. 'When we have finished this plan, it is going to help you and your team realize how important you all are to our business. This will lead us to focus more clearly on our priorities, and allow all of us to enjoy our success.' (15 seconds)

3 **Structure** – this is the agenda that you will take them through. People listen best to stories if you tell them what the story is about. 'We are going to look at five areas:
 ● a reminder of what we seek to achieve
 ● what we have produced so far
 ● a sanity check on the key elements for each of your departments
 ● how this will help us improve our reporting processes
 ● agreeing an action plan to implement our plan.' (15 seconds)

A useful tip is to display the agenda on a flip chart to help your audience understand where you are taking them.

In your introduction you should explain how you are going to handle questions. On **Thursday**, under 'Engage with your audience', I will explain why my preferred option is to allow questions at any time for all but the largest audiences.

All three of these elements have to be present in your introduction, although their order can be varied. Some of the most powerful introductions that I have seen have started with the benefit – which makes the audience sit up and think, 'This is not all about them – it's about me!'

Don't feel compelled to use the specific words 'purpose', 'benefit' and 'structure'. There are plenty of alternatives. What's needed is to convey the spirit of these words and, as with other aspects of presentation, variety is the spice of life. So, for example, you could opt for 'we aim' instead of purpose, 'we will gain' instead of benefit and 'agenda' rather than structure.

If your first few words are to make a real impact, it is best if domestic arrangements, such as the location of fire escapes and toilet facilities, are handled by someone else, along with a few words of introduction about you and the session. If you have to do it yourself, make sure that you show a clear-cut distinction between these things and the powerful introduction that you have planned.

There is an old presentation saying, 'Never start with an apology'. There's no need to – unless there is a serious reason for doing so, like being late. If you are late you should learn to allow for more contingencies so that it doesn't happen again! It is so much better to start with a positive, and through the week I will offer you tips on how to do this.

If you're not ready, don't start

Before we look at the body of your presentation, let me share with you something that put off an extremely competent presenter in front of an international audience. She came to open up her (previously loaded) presentation and realized that her backroom staff had reloaded the wrong presentation. She tried to muddle through, before eventually apologizing and stopping to locate the correct file and start again. This very experienced presenter realized, as she never had before, that whatever the pressures, if you're not ready you don't start!

The body

All too often this *is* the presentation, because there is no introduction and no proper end! In my experience, this is the easy bit. If your preparation and Mind Map suggest that the material should be in – it's in! If it's not essential – it's out, because time is precious and you don't want to get a bad reputation by detaining busy people longer than is necessary.

Few people can absorb more than three or four ideas in any one sitting, so keep the key messages to a minimum, and support your ideas with information provided prior to the presentation or after it. The body is best restricted to a few clear, direct messages that are connected with suitable signposts.

No one ever complains about a speech being too short!

Ira Hayes, Second World War hero

You need to finish speaking before your audience finishes listening!

53

The end

This also has three parts, and all three have to be included if you are to finish on a high. I will continue the example about the business plan.

1 **Summary** – just as in a report summary, there is a brief summary of the key ideas from each section. 'So, you've seen where we've got to with our business plan; you've seen how it affects your department; you've seen how it will make our reporting more effective, and we've agreed who does what next and when.'
2 **Conclusion** – people think that summary and conclusion are the same. They are nothing like the same, but they are likely to be linked. This is your chance to offer your personal view, such as (there are no 'right' answers here), 'This is going to put all of us in control of our business, and allow us to manage it more easily.'
3 **More** – this could take many forms:
   - 'Any questions?'
   - 'Come and talk to me afterwards.'
   - 'A working party [which could have come from the action plan] will be formed.'
   - 'There will be a further meeting.'
   - 'Think about one or two points and email me next week.'

Before we leave the end, make sure that you finish on a high – it's what people remember. So the end could be as simple as, 'Let's hit our plan!'

I see experienced, supposedly smooth presenters cover the body of the presentation expertly, but omit one or more of the three elements of the introduction, and one of the three parts of the end. Your presentations will be so much more effective with all seven parts; with all of them you will be seen to be a more effective presenter – and you will get results.

Balance risk and reward

In your preparation you need to consider whether you have
an appropriate balance between risk and reward – between
things that may offer the prospect of big gains and things that
could torpedo your efforts. If you don't take risks with material
and ideas, you might bore your audience and fail to secure
the optimum result. If you take too many risks, you could lose
your audience. Before you finally settle on your structure,
ask yourself whether you are comfortable with the balance
between risk and reward.

Summary

A sound structure is probably the most significant factor in giving you the confidence to deliver effectively. In your first few words you need to show that you are clear about your purpose, explain what's in it for your audience, and map out what you are going to do with them. Such an introduction will do more for your confidence than a fancy suit or clever words. The body of your presentation looks after itself if your preparation has been thorough and logical. The most important thing about the body is that it should be no longer than is needed to get your message across. Your ending is as crucial as your introduction, and needs to be as punchy. It needs to contain summary, conclusion and more, but if you are feeling particularly adventurous – and can see the opportunity – you could change the order (doing things in an unusual order is an example of the trade off between risk and reward).

This chapter is crucial in highly competitive times when people are looking for someone to make a difference. Follow this structure and you are well on the way to becoming an outstanding presenter.

Questions

1. How do you best get your key messages across?
   a) Rely on a combination of handouts, slides and your voice. ❏
   b) Tell 'em once ❏
   c) Tell 'em twice ❏
   d) Tell 'em, tell 'em and tell 'em (in the introduction, in the body and at the end). ❏

2. Your introduction needs to contain:
   a) purpose ❏
   b) benefit ❏
   c) structure ❏
   d) all three. ❏

3. The body of your presentation:
   a) is the most important part of your presentation ❏
   b) is all your audience is interested in ❏
   c) only makes sense if the introduction and the end each contain three component parts ❏
   d) is capable of being a stand-alone presentation. ❏

4. Your first few words should be:
   a) low key, softly, softly ❏
   b) an explanation of what's in it for the audience ❏
   c) an apology for something ❏
   d) funny. ❏

5. A great way to show people where you are going is to:
   a) display the agenda on a flip chart, to one side, and periodically show your audience what you've covered and where you are going next ❏
   b) assume that they don't need to know, so just plough on ❏
   c) explain the agenda (structure) just once ❏
   d) presume that they know. ❏

6. The end of your presentation needs to contain:
   a) summary ❏
   b) conclusion ❏
   c) more ❏
   d) all three. ❏

7. It's important that your audience knows:
   a) when they will be free to go ❏
   b) how long they will have for breaks ❏
   c) how much time you have allocated to questions ❏
   d) all of these things. ❏

8. Your summary and your conclusion amount to the same thing.
   a) true ❏
   b) dangerously untrue ❏
   c) false ❏
   d) almost true ❏

9. A three-part introduction and a three-part end are:
a) essential for audience engagement and for your success ☐
b) desirable ☐
c) optional ☐
d) painful. ☐

10. Good structure comes from:
a) your skill on the day ☐
b) a Mind Map or some similar preparation tool ☐
c) picking a few key areas within the subject ☐
d) luck. ☐

THURSDAY

Engage your audience

When making presentations, as in everyday life, it is very easy to speak *at* someone. Powerful communicators don't do that – they engage with people. I could have called this chapter 'Have a conversation', because that is what you need to do to engage with your audience. Throughout this book, from Sunday to Saturday, there are tips that will allow you to engage your audience, but this is so important that I choose to devote a chapter to it. It does mean that there is an element of (justifiable!) repetition of items that are touched on here and elsewhere. If I don't catch you on **Tuesday** I will catch you on **Sunday**!

The requirement is to make your audience think it's about them. If you involve them and carry them with you, you will achieve your objectives. You will shift them from State A to State B. Body language is an important part of engagement – a smile is an obvious example, but there are other aspects of this that we need to look at. Questions engage people, so we will look at how you can use questions to good effect – you asking the audience questions, and handling questions *from* the audience.

Today is a crucial day in you becoming an effective presenter!

I have come across many people who can deliver a speech (such as a best man or bride's father speech), yet they are poor at making a business presentation. Why is this? I feel it is because the speech is very much a one-way affair. It almost doesn't matter who's in the audience – you're going to get the speech as per the notes in the speaker's hand. In the worst type of speeches it's almost as if you are not real individuals – you are a lump of people who just happen to be in the same room. It's a very mechanical affair. I call this presenting *at*.

Your business presentation is an altogether different affair. Time is precious, so your audience expects you to relate to them quickly, and will consider you a failure if you don't. You will often know your audience extremely well, so you are under pressure to deliver a clearly understood result. You may be seriously challenged. You will need to be flexible enough to change your approach when things don't go quite to plan. So you need to touch each member of the audience as an individual, and having a conversation is the way to do it.

Don't despair! This is not a problem but an opportunity. If you apply the ideas outlined today, you will stand head and shoulders above most presenters. I offer you the visual below and a selection of my favourite tips on how to engage your audience. If the visual doesn't do the job, the tips will!

Have a conversation

Present *at* – no!　　　　　　　　　　　　　　Engage your audience – yes!

Shift your thinking from presenting to engaging.

Have a conversation

A selection of tips to help you engage with your audience:

- Don't do it because I say so. Do it because you want to do it. Do it because it works!
- If you start with the end in mind, as recommended on **Sunday**, you will already be thinking how your audience feels about the subject.

- Remember **Monday**'s message. You begin to engage with your audience when you realize that there is a presenting opportunity.
- Surprise, surprise, come **Tuesday**'s preparation there is a massive opportunity to ensure engagement. When you consider all those aspects of the audience that we looked at, you are laying the foundation that allows you to understand your audience, and relate to them.
- Seize an opportunity to gather audience expectations of you and your presentation.
- On **Wednesday**, your structure includes 'Tell them what's in it for them' when you sell the benefit. Today we are working on engagement as a separate subject, and come **Saturday** we will still be working on it. To succeed with presenting you never stop engaging your audience. It's not a technique – it's an attitude of mind!
- When you are about to present, don't wait for the audience to come to you – go and shake their hand. Acknowledge them if there are lots of them.
- Tell your audience what you expect of them. Do you want them to ask questions, take notes, chip in with their own experiences, buy something, come to a decision, or perform a task? Whatever you expect of them, explain it in your introduction.
- Avoid giving the audience the impression that you are reading a script. Make sure they perceive that you are having a conversation with them.
- Let your body do the talking; let it dance in tune with your words. Body language (see below) is a crucial part of intimacy.
- Ask plenty of questions and handle questioners sensitively.
- Use plenty of 'join' words – us; we; together. This gives everyone in the room a sense of unity.
- Use their jargon, examples that relate to them.
- Project to the whole room systematically, so everyone feels involved. You may find it helps to divide the room into sections, and look at one person in each section as you go round the room. Then go round the room again, looking at different people in each section.

- Be careful with humour, and stick to things you know will amuse your audience more than you! Move on quickly if your intended joke doesn't produce a laugh.

- Be sensitive to your audience. Check that their lightbulbs are coming on. If you need to, change the running order; change your use of visual aids; if things are not going as well as you want – change something!

Body language – use it!

Body language could be a book in its own right. Today we will only consider a few of the key tips that will help you get your message across, but first let's look at what would be suggested by many communications experts: when it comes to getting your message across, what you say is not as important as you think it is.

What you say = 10% of your impact

How you say it = 40% of your impact

Body language = 50% of your impact

Due to this, presenting an idea over the phone is a real challenge, because half of your communication toolkit is not available to you.

If you are sceptical about these numbers, I will not seek to convince you – although you may benefit from doing a search on the subject. I will simply ask you to consider that words are not as important as you think they are. This has huge implications for your delivery. You rarely need to put yourself under pressure to remember a sequence of words. The requirement is to get your message across – and how you say the words, together with your body language, is an important part of that.

Your presentation toolkit needs to make serious use of body language, so here are a few tips that might encourage you to study the subject in more detail:

- Smile. This is the shortest of the tips, but it has huge positive implications when it comes to relating to your audience. Smile when you enter the room and when you start. Smile regularly, even when you are asked tricky questions.
- Make regular eye contact with everyone in a small meeting, and scan the room comprehensively if it's a large gathering. This will give you the confidence that comes with knowing that you have made a connection. Eye contact is essential if you are to get your message across, but you need to get the balance right: too little eye contact and you appear nervous or shifty; too much and you seem intimidating or threatening. (This is one of many areas where doing something is a good idea, but if you overplay it you will lose any benefit. Asking too many questions of your audience would be another example of this.)
- Make your gestures larger than life. Not ridiculously so, but dramatic enough to be noticed rather than lost among the proceedings (for example, lean forward to accentuate a point, and make sure that the lean is noticed; thump the table to accentuate a point).
- Facial expressions are a good way of conveying what you feel about something, so as well as a smile, try a frown, a look of surprise or a look that shows you are questioning something. Reveal something of your emotions.
- During a short exchange or question, you might move to one side to show that you are relinquishing control to your audience. You step to the front to regain control.
- You might sit down to encourage a short debate, and stand up again to make it clear that you wish to move on.

- If you open your hands and turn them upwards, you are liable to be considered honest and allied to the group you are presenting to.
- Palms down gives people the impression that you have authority and will exercise power. This gesture could reinforce you saying 'No way!' because the words and the action go together.
- The way you organize seating makes a huge difference to the atmosphere in a room. A lecture style is the stuffiest, while the most open would be arranging chairs in a circle. A boardroom U layout allows you to get close to everybody if you walk down the middle of the U (all part of adding variety to maintain interest), and a few round tables is even more intimate – especially if you walk among them.
- Try to avoid having a barrier between you and your audience. Open spaces, allowing you to move around, are more conducive to engagement than lecture stands and tables.
- Make all your movements natural, but sufficiently emphasized to allow your audience to see them.
- There is the classic question of how to stop fiddling with the coins in your pocket. Some would argue that you shouldn't put your hands in your pockets at all. I feel that in moderation this is acceptable, even desirable if you are encouraging people to relax. As for the coins, the answer lies in the rest of this book – if you are presenting effectively, your nerves will be under control and you won't jangle the coins!

Choose your key words

I'm not saying that words are not important. A well-chosen word can have enormous impact on an audience, as can the order in which you use words. 'This car is cheap to run because it does 50 mpg' is less powerful than, 'It does 50 mpg, so it will save you money' because the audience will tend to remember the last few words, and saving money is what really appeals to them.

Think about the most powerful words in the English language, and use some of them – easy, simple, new, money, safe, secure, protected, save, retain, health, strength, results, benefits, discover, free, promise and guarantee. Use these words in your presenting, and roll them together for maximum impact: 'New ways to save you money'. One of the best ways to use key words is to be aware of the key words on each visual that you use. Not only will this make you realize what the key words are (you could make them bold), it will prompt you to cut unnecessary words from your visual.

Unless you really do want to alert people to a danger, use the positive more than the negative. So if you are, for instance, presenting how a change should be explained, avoid 'Don't be worried if this approach causes your people to become resentful' because you have planted a negative image in their brain! It's much better to say, 'If you want a positive response to this idea, explain how this will work for them.'

Use the active rather than the passive sense. 'Use short sentences' is likely to grab your audience's attention more than, 'Short sentences should be used.' (It's also a lot easier for you to remember, and to say.) 'What I would like to do' is less positive than 'What we will do'. Use 'prevent' not 'preclude'; 'ask' not 'request'. You choose – but it makes a difference!

'Dream' is an innocuous enough word, but when Martin Luther King said, 'I have a dream' it inspired millions, so I'm not saying that words aren't important – only that when communicating with others we tend to overestimate their importance and underestimate the impact of how they are said and of our body language. Martin Luther King reminds me that it is important not to swallow the ends of your words, or allow them to tail off. He hung on to the 'I - -' and the 'd- r- e- a- m'. You need to do the same for maximum impact. Another way of looking at this is to enunciate key words by opening your mouth more precisely than you would in normal speech. TV presenters do this all the time in order to give key words added weight.

Vary the style of your words

On **Tuesday** we looked at ways to vary your communication style. Varying the sort of words you use is essential if you are to engage all of your audience. Here are just a few examples of the sort of words that will appeal to those with different preferences:

● Audio types will appreciate: 'sounds okay'; 'that rings a bell'; 'can't hear above all this noise'.
● Visual types will prefer: 'That looks good'; 'I see that clearly'; 'what a great picture'.
● The feeling types will respond to: 'That feels great'; 'there's a tension in the air'; 'we're together on this'.

Ask questions of your audience

One certain way of engaging your audience is to ask them questions. Your core questions need to be built into your presentation, while others will crop up as you gauge audience reaction to your suggestions. The duration of your presentation will be seriously affected by any questions you ask, so you need to decide whether you want to ask a question and immediately answer it yourself (a rhetorical question), whether you want one person to answer, or whether you want a debate. In short, you need to decide how to control the question from start to finish, and indicate how you wish to move on. Here are some more tips on how to make questions work for you:

● Ask questions that you know are important to the audience. Not too clever, not an insult to their intelligence, but at the right level for them. You could ask one at the start.

- When you ask a question you are, in a sense, handing over control to someone else. You need to make it clear that you are doing this – by moving to one side for instance, or sitting down (see 'Body language' above).
- Build in a minimum number of questions to ask the audience (questions that they ask you are covered below). It's difficult to generalize on this, but I feel I've missed a trick if I don't ask at least three significant questions in a ten-minute presentation.
- To engage your audience, consider answering questions after each key section.

Handle questions with confidence

If someone in your audience asks a question, they are engaged, so welcome it. It takes courage for some people to ask a question (it's a form of public speaking to them), so the last thing you should do is put them down. Thank them, and ask yourself why they have chosen to ask the question, before you respond to them.

The courageous presenter will invite people to ask questions at any time (unless time or the size of the audience are a problem) and be skilled enough to manage it in a flexible way. If you don't trust yourself to handle questions when you are in full flow, then leave them to the end – but in the long term (see **Saturday**) develop your skills so that you can take questions at any time. There are very few situations where you can justify a one-way hurling of information at people, so don't just leave questions to the end. Inviting your audience to ask questions is the ultimate way to connect with them. To engage your audience, treat them as you would like to be treated in order not to fall asleep in someone else's presentation:

- Give some thought to the questions people might ask, and your likely response.
- In your introduction (the 'structure' part), explain how you would like questions to be handled, the stages at which they might be asked, and when you might answer them.
- Recognize that you will turn some people off if you don't answer their questions on the spot.
- Recognize that you could reduce the pressure on you if you do defer the answer.
- With a complex subject, if audience understanding is in doubt, summarize each key section and allow questions after each section. There is no point in proceeding if you've lost your audience! Checking their understanding will engage your audience and give you the confidence to proceed.
- Demonstrate that you have listened to the question. You could even repeat it: 'Thank you, Sam, I was hoping someone would ask me that. So you would like me to explain how this affects the sales team.'
- Pause. It shows that you have given a question proper consideration. Pauses are powerful. When you control the silence, you control the room!

The most precious thing in speech is a silence.

Sir Ralph Richardson, actor

- Don't just answer the questioner – answer the room, because you want to influence everyone.
- Bounce the question off everyone in the room: 'What does everyone think of that?' A variation on this is to invite people

to discuss the question among themselves in twos or threes, and then gather the responses from each group.

- Deal with the person before you deal with the question. One way of doing this is to allow someone to 'blow off steam' before addressing their question.
- Be honest, or you are likely to fail. If you don't know the answer, can anyone in the room answer the question for you? Do you need to come back to it later? (It could become part of 'more' in the end section of your presentation.)
- Check that the questioner is happy with your response
- Build in some contingency time for questions – whether you ask them, your audience asks them, or there is a question and answer session at the end. It might be a good idea to leave one part of the topic until the questions at the end!
- Allow due time for questions, but don't let them de-rail you. Assertively manage the time that is devoted to each question, and stick to the point with your answer.

If it's not working – change it!

This is another fundamental principle of business success that is also important to you during your presentation. You will sense how your audience is responding. If the reaction is good, consider doing even more of the same – for example using more visual aids if one has just gone down well (you could use your reserve material). If the reaction is lifeless, ask more questions or increase the pace of your delivery.

Summary

Presenting *at* people doesn't work in business presentations. You are unlikely to enjoy being talked at, and neither will your audience. You are working with them, working through them towards specific goals that affect you all. So you need to connect with all of your audience and engage them.

There are many tips to help you in this respect, but the most important is that you should want to connect in the fullest sense of the word. Your body language is important. So too are the questions you build in, and the way you encourage and handle questions from your audience. Above all, you will engage your audience if you put aside the idea of presentations being formal, and instead, however big the audience, have a conversation with them.

SUNDAY

MONDAY

TUESDAY

WEDNESDAY

THURSDAY

FRIDAY

SATURDAY

Questions

1. The best way of avoiding speaking *at* your audience is to:
   a) talk to the floor ❑
   b) have a conversation with them ❑
   c) read from your notes ❑
   d) look over their heads. ❑

2. The best way to engage with your audience is to:
   a) buy them a ring ❑
   b) think about their needs from the start of your preparation to the end of your delivery ❑
   c) crack a joke ❑
   d) agree with every questioner ❑

3. What is the most courageous approach to handling questions?
   a) Don't mention how and when you will take questions. ❑
   b) Restrict them to the end. ❑
   c) Allow questions at any time. ❑
   d) Make it clear you don't want any questions. ❑

4. What are you doing when you ask your audience a question?
   a) admitting that you've lost the plot ❑
   b) showing a weakness ❑
   c) being aggressive ❑
   d) temporarily handing over control ❑

5. Your carefully chosen words are:
   a) everything when it comes to getting your message across ❑
   b) the biggest factor in getting your message across ❑
   c) the second biggest factor ❑
   d) less important than how you say them and your body language. ❑

6. How long should eye contact last?
   a) until the other person gives in ❑
   b) until the other person realizes that you've looked at them ❑
   c) until you realize your eye contact has done its job ❑
   d) until you think you need to move on ❑

7. A silence:
   a) will make you feel uncomfortable ❑
   b) allows you to control your audience ❑
   c) suggests that you haven't prepared properly ❑
   d) shows that you are struggling. ❑

8. Who will you project to?
   a) the whole of your audience ❑
   b) your favoured few contacts ❑
   c) people at the front ❑
   d) those naturally in your eye line ❑

9. When is the best time to check that your audience is still with you?
   a) never, because there just isn't time ☐
   b) halfway through ☐
   c) at the end ☐
   d) at pre-planned times, plus whenever you sense the need ☐

10. Engagement with your audience stops when:
   a) you think you've done the job ☐
   b) all the key parties agree that the project is completed ☐
   c) you decide you've had enough ☐
   d) they make it quite clear that they've had enough. ☐

FRIDAY

More ideas for your toolkit

Today we are going to look at several aspects of presenting that are hugely important. In this toolkit we will consider how to manage your time in a way that suits you and your audience. We will look at the different types of memory aids available to you, and how to get them to work for you as you move through your presentation. We will consider how to make the best use of visual aids, including PowerPoint and flip charts, as well as developing a checklist to make sure that you take all the props you will need. You will see why PowerPoint doesn't make a presentation, but merely enhances it – and why our first five days were so crucial.

Treasure time

There are several aspects of time management that are worth thinking about:

- Preparation (**Tuesday**) is the key to managing your time successfully.
- When you rehearse, rehearse the timings. Then anticipate that your actual delivery will take longer, because you will elaborate, probably slow down your speech, and be slowed by interruptions.
- Rehearse your pauses.

> ***The right word may be effective, but no word was ever as effective as a rightly timed pause.***
>
> Mark Twain, author

- Have a clear strategy for dealing with interruptions. Ask people to ensure that you will not be interrupted, or channel interruptions through someone acting as a gatekeeper.
- Avoid showing films in a darkened room immediately after lunch. That's the time to engage your audience in an energizing activity.
- The most important thing is for you to recognize how long you need in order to make your case. People invariably take longer than is necessary, and longer than the audience want them to. Why? Usually because they are besotted with the subject, when they should be besotted with the audience and their needs.

Don't take longer than necessary

During the Second World War, Churchill instructed his staff to restrict their meeting minutes to one side of A4. He was the audience, and that was his clear expectation. I regularly explain to groups I work with that if they are given 60 seconds to sum up the history of the world, then that's all they've got! If you take longer than your audience wants you to take, you are shooting yourself and your chances in the foot.

- Rather unflatteringly, some people might like to know before you start what time they will get away. Tell them!
- Gathering a clear expectation of how long your audience is prepared to devote to a session is always a good idea. You might then take a conscious decision to steal a few more minutes, but be aware that you risk losing your audience.
- If things are going well, but you sense that you need more time, seek permission from your audience rather than spoil your good work.
- Have a clock close by when you rehearse and when you deliver. This allows you to check your progress against your planned schedule. Also, when you look at your clock there is some benefit in showing your audience that you are conscious of your time and respecting theirs.

Use memory aids to help you

A memory aid is anything that helps you to communicate smoothly and effectively. It's anything that moves you away from reading a script. They take many forms:

- Your presentation itself is the most obvious memory aid. It will work best for you and your audience if there are just a few key words to digest.
- Cue cards are the most traditional memory aid, but there are others. The fewer cue cards you need, the more fluent your delivery will be, because you will not be constantly looking at them.
- If you are using a quote, consider reading it from your cue card. It is acceptable to read a quote, and it takes the

pressure off you. The same is true of statistics that you want to get exactly right.

- Use a cue card to remind you of a question you want to ask the audience. Put them on postcards rather than on A4 sheets which do not look very professional.
- Clip your cards together to avoid getting confused.
- In a properly structured presentation, your last slide should lead you neatly on to the next one.
- A pencil note on the corner of a flip chart (invisible to the audience) can remind you what to do next.

Here's how to make best use of memory aids:

- Prepare, so you need to rely on them less!
- Have a clear structure so that it is obvious to you what comes next. A theme is a memory aid; it helps you through the presentation and also allows your audience to make sense of it.
- Have just a few big, bold words for any cue. Avoid sentences, otherwise there will be too many words and you won't be able to find the cue and will lose eye contact. The secret is to have enough information to trigger your memory, but not so much that you can't find the bit you want.
- Write messages that only you can see; pause; show surprise; ask a question.
- Be prepared to show that you are making limited use of your memory aids. There is no shame in this!

There is no 'best' memory aid – only one that works best for you and your audience.

Use visual aids to help your audience

We have already discussed the fact that the human brain responds well to being stimulated by visual aids and feeling things as well as by audio input. A mix allows better understanding, helps messages stick in the memory, grabs attention, helps the audience organize their thoughts, and can clearly demonstrate a sequence.

Make them big, **bold** and bright.

Don't use supporting materials just to be clever; only use them if they improve your ability to communicate your message. Just like structure, they are an essential part of grabbing your audience's attention and helping them to understand your message.

Flowcharts are particularly good at demonstrating chronological steps. Pie charts and bar charts are particularly effective at showing relationships between percentages and numbers. A datum line can usefully show the relationships between a base condition and other, different, situations. Models, videos, samples, photographs, drawings, brochures and handouts all have a place. Make sure that visual aids can be seen by everybody in the room, and avoid distractions like spelling mistakes.

There is always a debate about whether to distribute handouts during a presentation. They can generate interest from your audience, but they can also be a distraction that causes your audience to miss the next points you make. My rule on this is to only dish out handouts when the audience numbers are low enough for you to realize when you have 'lost' someone. At that point you can ask them a question to drag them back to you, or ask them to tear their eyes away from the handout. I offer handouts during a presentation to an audience of eight or fewer. With more than that, I would leave them to the end or use some other graphic. Another alternative is to pass round a visual aid, and wait for it to come back to you before proceeding.

Make layout part of your message, so the most important parts are at the top and on the left-hand side.

We are going to look in some considerable detail at PowerPoint and flip charts, but the principles involved in using them is the same – use them to support your message and, above all, use variety to keep your audience interested throughout.

Avoid death by PowerPoint

I've offered a few words of warning about PowerPoint, but let me leave you in no doubt – I believe that PowerPoint, properly used, is one of the most powerful presenting aids. The problem is that it is not always used wisely. Too often, people think that PowerPoint *is* the presentation, and this results in the audience switching off when the laptop is fired up. Every time you think of PowerPoint, pinch yourself to ensure that you make good use of it! Excessive reliance on this tool is bad for the presenter, and a total turn-off for the audience. My view is supported by two quotes:

> *Death by PowerPoint is the sick feeling that overcomes you when someone whips out their laptop. The level of resentment against slide show monotony is tangible. Some directors have banned the software, preferring their managers to summarize bullet points on a sheet of A4.*
>
> *Daily Telegraph*, February 2000
> (Churchill made the same point to his war cabinet.)

> *Many people use PowerPoint as a drunk uses a lamppost – more for support than illumination.*
>
> *People Management*, September 2002

The fact that these quotes are over ten years old makes this point even more relevant. These feelings have only got worse!

More positively, there is scope for using other presentation aids (flip charts are good) and, if you do use PowerPoint wisely, you and your presentation will be appreciated and well received.

Use PowerPoint effectively

- Recognize that there are plenty of software programmes that offer an alternative to PowerPoint. Just search the web for these.
- Use the flexibility that PowerPoint gives you to amend your presentation by changing the images, videos, words, layout, etc. at short notice.
- Design your slides after you have designed your presentation. PowerPoint isn't your presentation – it merely supports the key ideas. It is most powerful when used sparingly, with variety and in such a way that it allows you to have a conversation.
- Don't think that PowerPoint allows you to present someone else's presentation – present your ideas in your way.
- Use slides to support your ideas and add to them – not as a script to read from. Recognize that the human brain has this wonderful ability to multitask. It is quite capable of listening to you, seeing just a few words on the screen and watching you use a model at the same time. If you resort to reading too many words from the screen you will lose eye contact with your audience, and you might as well just email them your notes. Resist the temptation for your slides to say everything that you do!
- Avoid jargon, just as you do when you speak.
- Use simple headlines that signpost what's on the slide, rather than compete with the words.
- Keep the whole thing simple – use a few words and a couple of fonts. Five lines of text or five bullet points are usually enough. Use it to support your point, not to make your point. Avoid fancy animation, reveals and slide transitions that are too clever and too repetitious. With this tool, less is more!
- Insert pictures rather than words – they are more memorable. Consider using them on their own, with no text.

- Resist the temptation to import blocks of text – text is meant for reading in a document, not on a screen. Spreadsheets are to be avoided unless you are presenting to one person and have plenty of time.
- Give the text a chance – don't clutter up slides with a logo on each one.
- Vary the layout to reduce boredom and maintain interest – don't always use bullet points; sometimes reveal a line at a time; sometimes reveal a page at a time.
- Consider building a slide in several stages. Stage 1 could be just one word or line. Stage 2 could be a picture added to the one line. Stage 3 could add the final line to the same slide.
- Reinforce your message with copies of your slides in any handouts you distribute.
- Make sure that you have a contingency plan to cover the projector or the software failing. A set of handouts is an obvious backup.
- Use your keyboard! The slide number plus 'Enter' will take you to a particular slide. One of my favourites is to use PowerPoint to maximize my initial impact by setting up my first slide and then pressing 'B'. The screen goes blank, and you are in control of when the audience sees your first image. When you are ready, press 'B' again to restore the image. You'll start with a bang. I am always astonished how few presenters know how to use this powerful tip.

Use the power of flip charts

One of the most powerful presentations that I ever saw was from a Jaguar executive who shared with 60 of us how Jaguar had been restructured. He could only cope with such a number by working with two flip charts on an elevated stage, but he succeeded because he used all the tricks of the flipchart wizard. He sought to share his experiences with us in the hope that we would be able to use some of these Jaguar ideas. He succeeded because he:

- communicated his key messages with conviction
- used BIG images

- kept to a handful of key areas in his presentation
- maintained eye contact when pointing to the flip chart
- kept silent when he drew images (which I discovered subsequently he had faintly sketched in with a pencil so that we couldn't see the draft image)
- moved to a blank sheet while we had a discussion – rather than leave an irrelevant sheet in full view (the equivalent tip with PowerPoint is to press 'B' to blank the slide while you are promoting a discussion)
- never stood between us and his visual aid; he always gave us a clear view of the image he was referring to

These are simply good practice with any visual aid, but they really worked well in a situation where most people would have struggled to use a flip chart. As a result, the friendliness, intimacy and improvisation a flip chart allows was put to good use.

To the above suggestions on flip charts I would add these suggestions for a smaller audience:

- Number the pages just like you would number PowerPoint slides, to allow you to locate them at question time.
- Have pre-prepared blobs of Blu-Tack or similar adhesive ready so you can take a sheet off and display it to one side. This is particularly useful with something like an agenda, which can be permanently displayed so you can periodically show your audience where you've got to and what's coming next (PowerPoint doesn't allow you to do this).

SUNDAY MONDAY TUESDAY WEDNESDAY THURSDAY FRIDAY SATURDAY

Develop your own checklist of props

This is part of your preparation, but **Tuesday** was already a big chapter! I always refer to a checklist of the things that I must remember to take, and do a final check that everything is there before loading the car. It only takes a few minutes to compile, and you can add to it as you learn what's important to you. I won't give you my complete list, because the real value comes in developing your own – then you don't forget anything. Here are a few from my list to set you on the way:

- Laptop
- TV
- Camcorder
- Projector
- DVDs
- Extension cables
- Handouts
- Sets of contingency handouts
- Samples
- Cue cards
- Blu-tack
- Spare flip chart
- Personal notes
- Info on company
- List of contacts
- Lunch – time?
- Coffee break a.m.
- Water/biscuits
- Coffee break p.m.
- When will you have access to the room?

Such a list allows you to check not only what you need to take, but also what you will need in the room. It will prompt you to agree with your host what will be available to you. The end result is less hassle, no last-minute panics, and you in the right frame of mind to communicate.

Build in contingencies

This is another area that needs to be considered at the preparation stage.

If anything happens to disturb your equilibrium, you will be thrown off track and your chosen goals will be at risk. You need to build in contingencies at every stage if you are to present with a clear head. Here are a few suggestions:

● However long you think it will take you to travel, allow a bit more time for hold-ups.
● Consider travelling the night before.
● However long you think it will take to set up, add some time in case the set-up doesn't run as smoothly as you'd hoped.
● Have a plan for what you will cut if you start running out of time.
● Have a different plan to cope with your audience being ready to spend extra time on a particular subject. A useful idea here is to have discretionary material up your sleeve – then use it if the situation presents itself.

Preparation is important, but don't ever expect a presentation to go to plan. A prime function of your preparation is to allow you to cope with anything that happens! You should always be flexible, and contingency planning allows you to cope with the unexpected.

Consider co-presenting

We have looked at how important variety is if we are to keep our audience interested, and so far we have considered you being the only presenter. If you want to introduce variety, why not have a co-presenter? Why do TV channels like the BBC, ITV and Sky use two presenters so often? It's because it works! Two presenters can communicate better than one. If you present alongside someone, you can get a feel for audience reaction while your colleague is presenting. Your audience will listen afresh, and you can collect your thoughts ready for when your next slot comes around. There are a few things that you have to manage with this approach:

- You need to rehearse that bit more to ensure smooth transitions.
- This is especially true if you extend this idea to a team presentation of three or more.
- You need to work well together, complement each other.
- You need to present a united front working towards a common goal.
- You need to agree clear responsibilities. Who does what? Who answers which questions?

You also need to consider the wider situation within which you are asked to present:

- You may be asked to present between two other people as one of a series of presentations, in which case you need to be aware of their style and their messages.
- Your presentation may be followed by a panel discussion, in which case it would be a good idea to know the panel's views.
- You might be invited to present a guest slot in another department's monthly meeting, in which case you need to know the objectives of your sponsor and any special issues of the moment.

In all these cases there is an added dimension to knowing the outputs/objectives, and reading your audience so that you achieve your goals.

Summary

This toolkit starts with how to manage time successfully. Not only should you plan the timing of your presentation, you should rehearse it, complete with an allowance for questions – and even pauses!

Memory aids support you as you move through your presentation. They can take many forms. The 'right' ones are the right ones for you – the ones that move you confidently and smoothly from one section to another without your audience thinking it's a big deal.

Be sure to avoid death by PowerPoint, and use the tips on how to use, rather than abuse, this powerful tool. The most important tip is to use it, not shelter behind it.

I invite you to build up your own checklist of what needs to be in the room when you present; making sure that all these props and facilities are there is an important part of you being in the right frame of mind to make an impact with your introduction. Allow for contingencies – otherwise you will be thrown off track. Finally, you might consider taking the pressure off yourself by working with a co-presenter.

SUNDAY

MONDAY

TUESDAY

WEDNESDAY

THURSDAY

FRIDAY

SATURDAY

Questions

1. Your presentation timings could go wrong if:
   a) your audience realizes that you are anxious about the time ❏
   b) you rehearse in the room, complete with all your kit ❏
   c) you rehearse the pauses ❏
   d) you pack in every conceivable aspect of the subject. ❏

2. What is the best way to manage interruptions?
   a) Go with the flow, let it happen. ❏
   b) Explain your approach to interruptions before you start; have a strategy. ❏
   c) Ban all interruptions. ❏
   d) Deal with each interruption as it happens. ❏

3. Avoiding memory aids, and relying on a phenomenal memory, will:
   a) show that you are very clever ❏
   b) ensure that you will get it right ❏
   c) put you under unnecessary pressure ❏
   d) mean you have to rehearse less. ❏

4. The best way to remember to ask the audience a question is to:
   a) keep it in your head ❏
   b) rehearse it dozens of times ❏
   c) build it in using a cue card or some other memory aid ❏
   d) rely on the subject area cropping up. ❏

5. How can you reduce the number of prompts that you need?
   a) Rehearse until you are fed up with rehearsing. ❏
   b) Relax and rely on getting it right. ❏
   c) Put absolutely everything on your visual aids. ❏
   d) Have a simple, clear structure that reveals an obvious thread. ❏

6. What is the best way to ensure that you get your message across?
   a) Use a balance of all three forms of communication. ❏
   b) Design great visual aids. ❏
   c) Appeal to people's emotions. ❏
   d) Use powerful words. ❏

7. To use handouts effectively:
   a) leave them to the end ❏
   b) dish them out widely in the room ❏
   c) pass them round and wait for them to come back to you ❏
   d) judge each situation on its merits. ❏

8. PowerPoint slides work best if:
   a) you vary your approach to support your key messages ❏
   b) each slide has the same layout ❏
   c) your slides drive your presentation ❏
   d) you make sure your logo is on every slide. ❏

9. What's the biggest problem with flip charts?
a) People can't read them. ❏
b) They are untidy. ❏
c) They get in the way. ❏
d) You fail to recognize their power. ❏

10. What's the best way to make sure you take with you everything that you need?
a) Put everything in boxes. ❏
b) Prepare it the night before. ❏
c) Develop your own checklist to make sure you leave nothing behind. ❏
d) Rely on your memory. ❏

SATURDAY

Continuously improve your performance

> ***There are always three speeches for every one you gave – the one you practiced; the one you gave; and the one you wish you'd given.***
>
> Dale Carnegie, author of *How to Win Friends and Influence People* – the first business book I ever read; I'm still working on this!

There is a fine balance to be struck between confidence and arrogance; between being organized and being flexible; between trusting yourself and continuously improving your performance. We finish the week with some ideas on developing your skills as a presenter. You have a toolkit in this book that has equipped you to be a competent presenter. Now we have to ensure that you are perceived by those around you as an outstanding communicator – someone they want to work with!

In order to improve you have to learn, so we will look at the learning cycle. Feedback is the key to learning and improving your performance. You need feedback from people you can trust; before the event, from someone who will watch you rehearse; at the end of the event; and from your audience when they have had time to reflect. Finally, you need feedback from outside parties who have spoken to your audience and collected reactions to your efforts. From start to finish you should be taking stock of your own performance.

Before we set about making you outstanding, let's pause to consider whether everyone can present successfully. I have met very few people who can't, but occasionally I come across people who will never be convinced that they can do it. In such extreme cases there is no shame in admitting that you should leave it to others. For the vast majority, here are some ideas to turn you from good to outstanding.

Define the competent presenter skill set

Most actors say they are nervous, even sick with nerves, before going on stage. The way you are affected in this respect might never go away, but there is one thing you can work on, one thing you can exercise control over. That's you! And you can improve your performance by using this checklist. The simplest way to do this is to rate yourself out of 10 against each of the criteria below, and also ask your reviewers to rate you from 0 to 10.

1 How impressive was the opening? Purpose/benefit/ structure. Length? Impact?
2 Was there clear evidence of preparation? Reference the audience, yourself, your material.
3 Confidence level – how was it?
4 Structure – were all the elements present: introduction (PBS); body; end (SCM)?
5 How audience-friendly was the body?
6 Did your body language reinforce the message? Did you use movement? Expressions?
7 Eye contact – too much or too little? Just right? Evenly spread round the room?
8 Use of visual aids – was there variety/a mix of visuals? Clarity? Were sizes right?
9 Voice variation – were there changes of volume, pace, emphasis?
10 Natural manner – did you have a conversation?
11 Did you avoid a script?

12 Were there examples, analogies, stories and jargon related to the audience?

13 Did you ask questions? Enough? Related to the audience? Did you develop their answers?

14 Did you invite enough questions? Did you manage them successfully and check that the answers were well received?

15 Mannerisms and pet words (uhm, er, actually) – did you use too many? Did any put off the audience?

16 Empathy – did you put yourself in their shoes?

17 Was there humour? Enough? Too much? Did it work?

18 Enthusiasm – was there passion?

19 Did you control the total time? The time spent on questions?

20 Were key points well made? Repeated enough? Repeated too much?

21 Did you achieve your objectives?

This is a long list to manage, and it could be longer. Relax! You, and anyone reviewing your performance, can only sensibly focus on one, two or three of the most important areas of your development. Nobody can digest or develop more than that at any one time. You need to spot your most important development need, work on it, and then later move on to the next areas that can be improved.

At the same time, focus on being aware of your key strengths and boost your confidence by consciously putting these to good effect.

Don't get too technical about how you use this checklist. Use it in such a way that it suits you or anyone giving you feedback on your performance. Consider it as part of your personal development plan. Add other items to your skill set if you think they are a factor in your performance.

Realize how you learn

Kolb is usually credited with identifying that we all learn according to a learning cycle. You will learn to be a better presenter if you understand this cycle:

- Have an experience – of presenting.
- Review the experience – in your own mind and with others giving you feedback.
- Draw conclusions – decide what you will do about it.
- Plan the next practical step – have another go.
- Go round the loop again and again.

You learn at every stage as you go through the cycle, but you need to be aware that your reflection, and feedback from others, is crucial if your performance is to improve.

Honey and Mumford came up with a related idea – that we have different preferences when it comes to learning. Some of us prefer to learn by doing (activists), some by reflecting (reflectors), some by using theory (theorists), and some by

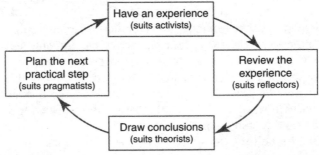

We all learn in these different ways at different stages in the cycle

The learning cycle

fitting it into the workplace (pragmatists). We all learn through all four routes, but we each have different preferences.

Identifying your own learning styles will enable you to play to your strengths (your strongest preference) and work on your least preferred style. That way you will become a more balanced learner, and as a result improve your presentation technique.

Make the most of the feedback you receive

If you are receiving feedback from someone, make sure that you make the most of it. I use a formula called EEC:

- *Example* – make sure they tell you exactly what you did, or specifically what happened.
- *Effect* – ask what effect that had on them
- *Change* – what needs to change to effect improvement OR
- *Continue* – keep it up if it's one of your strengths.

If you are reviewing your own performance, go through the formula in the same way to help you come up with specific things that you need to do to improve.

To get the best from this sort of feedback, here are a few more things worth doing:

- Be sure you listen before you interrupt.
- Don't be defensive. Understand what is being said and why.
- You don't have to agree with the feedback, but it will pay to seek specific examples of what the observer saw.
- Ask, 'Is there anything else I should be looking at in this same area?'
- Express your honest reaction to the feedback, and thank the giver.
- If you are feeling brave, ask for feedback from your audience at the end of your presentation.

Use the formula and tips above, and those giving you feedback will feel that it is valued, and you will go from strength to strength.

Check your attitude as well

Above I have invited you to check on your skills. That is extremely helpful, but if some of your attitudes are not right then it will be very difficult to improve your skills. So, ask yourself a few questions and be honest with yourself about the answers:

- Do you think you are okay? Are you happy to be you? Don't start till you're okay!
- Do you have a demon that you need to be honest about? Do you hate using a particular piece of equipment? Do you fear a particular type of person? If you do, you need to be honest about it and decide either to live with it or to address it as part of your development plan.
- Be honest with yourself about any of your mindsets that will inhibit you and adversely affect your performance. Do you have a problem with people of a certain status? Do you have a bias against a particular person, or towards a particular policy? These are perfectly human reactions, but if any of them get in the way of you performing well, you first need to be honest with yourself before deciding how to overcome them. As a young manager I had a fear of one particular director, and confided in my mentor at the time. She said, 'Picture him naked.' He looked ridiculous. The fear was gone!
- Do you *want* to step into the audience's shoes? Unless you are genuine about this, your audience will smell a rat. As you've already read, Mark Twain said, 'If you are to enter another person's shoes you must first take off your own.' So, don't start till you have taken off your own shoes.
- Do you believe in what you say? Again, don't start until you do because any lack of conviction on your part will torpedo your efforts. One way to stop negative messages undermining you is to link any bad news with compensating factors. For instance, acknowledging the cost of a product

is easier if you remind yourself and others that it will save money in the long run.

> **You will speak well if your tongue delivers the message of your heart.**
>
> John Ford, film director

● Does your belief show as passion? Your passion will carry your audience with you.

> **No person who is enthusiastic about his work has anything to fear from life.**
>
> Samuel Goldwyn, founder of several film studios, who left
> Warsaw as a young man, on foot and penniless

● Have you visualized success? Are you being positive about your approach to presenting? Picturing yourself succeeding is another example of starting with the end in mind, and is an essential foundation on which to improve your skills. Take a lead from the world's top sports stars. Their preparation involves them creating a mental picture of them winning. It's an important part of trusting yourself to deliver, and giving you the confidence you need

● Are you constantly on the lookout for improvements?

Video yourself

The most powerful thing you can do to improve your performance is to video yourself, or have someone else video you. Over many years I have found that however hard I try to give people feedback on how their messages are coming across, nothing carries as much weight as seeing and hearing yourself. Words alone cannot always convince someone that there needs to be more passion in their delivery, but a camcorder can. It's a great example of the audio, visual, kinaesthetic combination at work – we looked at this on **Tuesday**.

Move to unconscious competence

There is a model that sums up what you are doing as you continuously improve your performance. You are moving to a situation where top-level performance is second nature to you. You don't have to think about it, and you perform fluently. It's called the conscious competence model, and it is usually shown as a cycle. I prefer to show it as steps that lead you to a pinnacle:

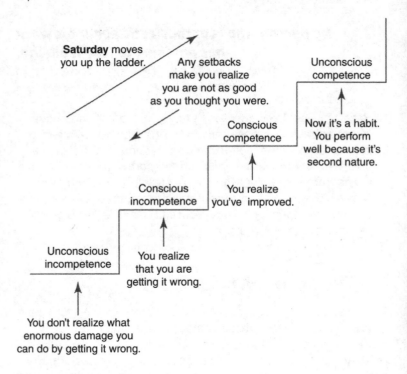

We could look at the development of any top sportsperson, but here we'll look at someone learning to drive a car:

1 **Unconscious incompetence** – you don't realize the terrible damage that you can do if you understeer, or brake too violently. Cars driven badly can kill!

2 **Conscious incompetence** – you begin to realize that your braking is too erratic, and could land you in trouble – you are aware of the consequences. Hopefully, at this stage you want to learn to do it better.

3 **Conscious competence** – feedback from others, or your own self-awareness, makes you realize that you have improved. You have just joined a motorway with more confidence.

4 **Unconscious competence** – you don't have to struggle with constant attention to technique. Good practice is deep in your subconscious. You are fluent and confident. You drive for ten miles without thinking about it, and you haven't had an accident.

Any failure at this stage drives you back down to conscious incompetence, and you have to climb the ladder again. As I write I am receiving coaching from the Institute of Advanced Motorists, working towards taking their test. I was horrified when my coach showed me that, judged by their high standards, I was an okay driver but not an advanced one. I need to change my technique, and need to unlearn the bad habits of many years before new techniques become second nature. It could well be two steps forward and one step back as I become a better driver and you become a better presenter!

Keep abreast of technology

It is important to keep up with technology, because (a) it can enhance your performance and (b) your audience will expect it. There will always be more and more aids that you can download from the internet to allow you to import software, video clips or stills. Powerful though they are, remember that they don't make a presentation – they merely help you to communicate your message more powerfully. Flip charts and the traditional visual aids such as a single-page handout or sample can be equally powerful. Variety, and an appropriate blend, is more important than gimmicks.

Start with the end goal in mind

On **Sunday** we started with the end goal in mind. We looked at the importance of preparation – clarifying the outputs that you want; preparing for your audience; preparing yourself; preparing your material. We looked at the different outputs you might seek or objectives to achieve – action; decisions; changing the way people feel about things; reaching a mutual understanding; generating ideas; or someone buying from you. We also covered the importance of not relying just on words to get your message across, but also appealing to emotions and to the visual sense. So here is a visual representation of all these ideas:

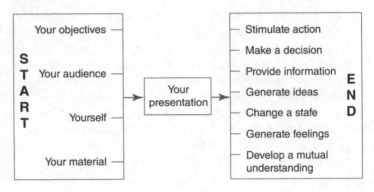

Summary

The challenge is to keep asking yourself, and those around you, two questions:

- What have I got to do more of?
- What have I got to do less of?

Then you are well placed to make yourself an even better presenter than you are now. Use the checklist to rate your performance from 0 to 10 and crystallize your thoughts on how to improve. Take a balanced view of how to make good use of your strengths as well as focusing on a few development needs at any one time.

Feedback is the key to this, and it needs to come from a combination of honest self-appraisal and the observations of a trusted friend, colleague or coach. Make sure the feedback is specific – along the lines of EEC – so that you can do something specific to improve your performance. Being honest with yourself will involve you questioning your attitudes as well as your skills, because things like your confidence, your passion and your inner beliefs will have more impact on your effectiveness than technique. Approach any presentation with the right attitude, keep developing your skills, keep abreast of

SUNDAY MONDAY TUESDAY WEDNESDAY THURSDAY FRIDAY SATURDAY

technology, and you will quickly be perceived as one of the most competent presenters around. And, importantly, start with an image of you presenting with confidence – start with the end in mind!

Good luck on your journey.

Questions

1. The best way to benefit from feedback on your performance is to:
a) secure it when you rehearse ❏
b) ask for it at the end of your presentation ❏
c) sit down with a trusted colleague ❏
d) use a blend of all three, depending on the situation and the time available. ❏

2. What is the most important aspect of gathering feedback from others?
a) people providing specific examples of what you did ❏
b) observations on how your attitudes showed themselves in your behaviour (were they helpful or unhelpful?) ❏
c) suggestions on how what you did affected your audience ❏
d) a combination of all three ❏

3. When gathering feedback you should:
a) listen carefully – look behind the words for the message ❏
b) understand not just what is being said, but why ❏
c) thank the giver for the feedback ❏
d) all of the above. ❏

4. To develop your presenting and communication skills you need to:
a) address the complete package of the competent presenter skill set ❏
b) have an interesting thread in the middle ❏
c) end on a positive ❏
d) find new ways of grabbing people's attention at the start. ❏

5. What is the most manageable way for you to improve?
a) Focus on the complete list of 20 plus items on the checklist. ❏
b) Be guided by your instinct. ❏
c) Be guided by a trusted colleague. ❏
d) Make sure that you only work on two, or a maximum of three, issues at any one time. ❏

6. Why do you need to be more aware of your attitudes than your skills?
a) Because skills are easier to change than attitudes. ❏
b) Because the way you behave is driven by your attitudes, so you need to understand your attitudes if you are to develop your skills in a positive way. ❏
c) Because attitudes are more complicated than skills. ❏
d) Because attitudes are hidden. ❏

111

7. Your attitudes will lead your audience to make judgements about:
a) your passion ❏
b) your sincerity ❏
c) your motives ❏
d) all three, and more besides. ❏

8. The best way to secure feedback on your performance is to:
a) trust your instincts ❏
b) have yourself videoed ❏
c) ask the audience ❏
d) rely on colleagues. ❏

9. Where do you want to be on the conscious competence model?
a) unconscious of your incompetence ❏
b) conscious of your incompetence ❏
c) conscious of your competence ❏
d) unconscious of your competence ❏

10. What will be the most important aspect of you moving to unconscious competence and communicating effectively with a wide range of people in different situations?
a) being super confident of your own ability ❏
b) being modest ❏
c) being genuinely committed to continuously improving your performance ❏
d) taking a balanced view of your attitudes and skill set ❏

Surviving in tough times

The real value of presenting becomes clear when you realize that you don't just do it when you are on your feet in front of a group. We present all the time, and we use our presenting skills when we sell, negotiate, fundraise, manage change, consult, seek to persuade, pass on information, communicate in meetings and communicate one-to-one. This is true in the private, public and voluntary sectors. Wherever you work, in tough times presenting your case effectively will give your organization a much-needed edge and improve your own prospects.

1 Make good use of time

From the top to the bottom of organizations people are under huge time pressure. If you are expert at presenting ideas and information it will save your senior managers considerable time. You will be seen to make a difference. Your contribution will be appreciated. Also, you will save yourself time and get better results if you present your case effectively at an appropriate time. This is true of so many situations, including when you are selling, influencing your department, influencing others and persuading in a one-to-one situation. It's a chance for you to stand out!

2 It will promote you!

Presenting will highlight your particular skills and help you get promoted. Presenting requires many of the core communication skills that are needed in business today. In tight times it is especially important to display creativity, clear thinking and energy, as well as time management, leadership and managerial skills. Presenting is an opportunity to put these skills in your shop window. It is also an opportunity for you to improve and develop those skills. Presenting promotes you!

3 Demonstrate high-level thinking

When everyone tends to get drawn into short-term action, the value of strategic thinking becomes more obvious. 'In the land of the blind, the one-eyed man is king.' Skilled preparation should allow you to pick out the key issues and build them into your presentation. Then, during the presentation itself, you can demonstrate this strategic thinking, how it will benefit the organization and how it will benefit your audience. Good structure is key if you are to influence high-level strategy. Follow the guidelines on structure in this book and you will make a vital difference.

4 Be seen to be an agent for positive change

Organizations have to change as never before. Standing still is not an option, so if your contribution is visibly moving things forward you will be well regarded. Whether your presentation is about changing the organization, changing perceptions or changing procedures, presenting is an opportunity for you to be appreciated. It's the clarity of your outputs that will lead to you and your ideas being valued.

5 Get a Job!

Increasingly employers are building presentations into their selection and assessment procedures. They do so with good reason, because you display a wide range of business skills when you present. If your would-be employer spots good communication skills, an ability to relate to others, clear thinking and an organized approach, you are halfway through the door. The approach outlined in this book will seriously increase your chances of ticking the interviewer's boxes and securing your next job, whether it is on internal or an external move.

6 Make people sit up and listen to you

If you gain a reputation for delivering clear messages when you present formally, you will be listened to more as you go about your business on a day-to-day basis. Most of the skills covered in this book have a part to play in helping you communicate effectively with those around you. It's easy. Use these skills to influence others, and get listened to!

7 Stay legal!

Possession may be nine tenths of the law. Presentation and communication is nine tenths of employment law, because on a day-to-day basis managers have to be aware of a host of industrial relations and health and safety issues. Explaining your ideas simply, clearly and within the law is an important part of safe management processes. Be appreciated as a safe pair of hands!

8 Sell more

Your customers are more discerning in tight times. They have more options than ever before, and they are looking for something special to convince them to buy from you.

Good presenting is a way of demonstrating the superiority of the products or service you are offering. This is true if you are selling one-to-one, bidding to several people or engaged in a tendering process. Effective presenting allows your key messages and very personal approach to come to the fore, inspiring confidence and securing more business.

9 Negotiate better deals

Presenting contributes hugely to successful negotiations. When you negotiate, you present your case. The better your case, the more it appeals to your audience; and the better your presentation of it, the more likely you are to reach a satisfactory agreement. It's another opportunity to make a significant difference!

10 Generate priceless data

To formulate sound strategies, policies and action we need reliable data. Presenting is a fabulous way of explaining to people what's happening, what you seek to do, why you seek to do it and what's in it for them. The better your explanation, the better will be their response. Your presentation of data gives you an opportunity to improve decision making within your organization. This is another area where the importance of a solid structure can easily be missed. Good structure allows dry data to be turned into better business. It's priceless!

Answers

Sunday: 1d; 2a; 3d; 4b; 5a; 6a; 7d; 8d; 9d; 10d.

Monday: 1d; 2b; 3a, 4d; 5d; 6c; 7c; 8d; 9b; 10d.

Tuesday: 1d; 2b; 3b; 4d; 5c; 6d; 7a; 8a; 9d; 10d.

Wednesday: 1d; 2d; 3c; 4b; 5a; 6d; 7d; 8b; 9a; 10b.

Thursday: 1b; 2b; 3c; 4d; 5d; 6c; 7b; 8a; 9d; 10b.

Friday: 1d; 2b; 3c; 4c; 5d; 6a; 7d; 8a; 9d; 10c.

Saturday: 1d; 2d; 3d; 4a; 5d, 6b; 7d; 8b; 9d; 10c.

Notes

ALSO AVAILABLE IN THE 'IN A WEEK' SERIES

For information about other titles in the series, please visit
www.inaweek.co.uk

ALSO AVAILABLE IN THE
'IN A WEEK' SERIES

SUCCESSFUL JOB APPLICATIONS • SUCCESSFUL JOB HUNTING
• SUCCESSFUL KEY ACCOUNT MANAGEMENT • SUCCESSFUL LEADERSHIP
• SUCCESSFUL MARKETING • SUCCESSFUL MARKETING PLANS
• SUCCESSFUL MEETINGS • SUCCESSFUL MEMORY TECHNIQUES
• SUCCESSFUL MENTORING • SUCCESSFUL NEGOTIATING • SUCCESSFUL
NETWORKING • SUCCESSFUL PEOPLE SKILLS • SUCCESSFUL
PRESENTING • SUCCESSFUL PROJECT MANAGEMENT • SUCCESSFUL
PSYCHOMETRIC TESTING • SUCCESSFUL PUBLIC RELATIONS •
SUCCESSFUL RECRUITMENT • SUCCESSFUL SELLING • SUCCESSFUL
STRATEGY • SUCCESSFUL TIME MANAGEMENT • TACKLING INTERVIEW
QUESTIONS

For information about other titles
in the series, please visit
www.inaweek.co.uk

LEARN IN A WEEK,
WHAT THE EXPERTS
LEARN IN A LIFETIME

For information about other titles
in the series, please visit
www.inaweek.co.uk